TABLE OF CONTENTS

CHAPTER 1

A BELL RINGS

It is four o'clock in London, England. A massive bell rings four times. People nine miles (14 kilometers) away can hear it! It is inside the clock at the top of Elizabeth Tower.

Elizabeth Tower

BIG BEN

by Kristine Spanier, MLIS

Ideas for Parents and Teachers

Pogo Books let children practice reading informational text while introducing them to nonfiction features such as headings, labels, sidebars, maps, and diagrams, as well as a table of contents, glossary, and index.

Carefully leveled text with a strong photo match offers early fluent readers the support they need to succeed.

Before Reading

- "Walk" through the book and point out the various nonfiction features. Ask the student what purpose each feature serves.
- Look at the glossary together. Read and discuss the words.

Read the Book

- Have the child read the book independently.
- Invite him or her to list questions that arise from reading.

After Reading

- Discuss the child's questions. Talk about how he or she might find answers to those questions.
- Prompt the child to think more. Ask: Big Ben and the clock tower are often shown in movies that take place in London. Have you ever noticed the tower in a movie?

Pogo Books are published by Jump!
5357 Penn Avenue South
Minneapolis, MN 55419
www.jumplibrary.com

Copyright © 2021 Jump!
International copyright reserved in all countries.
No part of this book may be reproduced in any form without written permission from the publisher.

Library of Congress Cataloging-in-Publication Data

Names: Spanier, Kristine, author.
Title: Big Ben / by Kristine Spanier.
Description: Minneapolis, MN: Jump!, Inc., [2021]
Series: Whole wide world | Includes index.
Audience: Ages 7–10 | Audience: Grades 2–3
Identifiers: LCCN 2020023885 (print)
LCCN 2020023886 (ebook)
ISBN 9781645277279 (hardcover)
ISBN 9781645277330 (paperback)
ISBN 9781645277286 (ebook)
Subjects: LCSH: Big Ben (Tower clock)–Juvenile literature.
Classification: LCC TS543.5.L6 S63 2021 (print)
LCC TS543.5.L6 (ebook)
DDC 681.1/130942132–dc23
LC record available at https://lccn.loc.gov/2020023885
LC ebook record available at https://lccn.loc.gov/2020023886

Editor: Jenna Gleisner
Designer: Molly Ballanger

Photo Credits: Lukas Holub/Shutterstock, cover; Ikpro/Shutterstock, 1; Sergey Novikov/Shutterstock, 3; Lana Yatsyuk/Shutterstock, 4; Jon Arnold Images Ltd/Alamy, 5, 11; Mistervlad/Dreamstime, 6-7; Atlaspix/Shutterstock, 7; chrisdorney/Shutterstock, 8-9; Still AB/Shutterstock, 10 (frame); Illustrated London News Ltd/Pantheon/SuperStock, 10 (image); Veja/Shutterstock, 12-13 (background); Art Collection 2/Alamy, 12-13 (foreground); Bruno Vincent/Getty, 14-15; Hulton Archive/Getty, 16-17; Heloise/Alamy, 18; oversnap/iStock, 19; 1000 Words/Shutterstock, 20-21; Voyagerix/Shutterstock, 23.

Printed in the United States of America at Corporate Graphics in North Mankato, Minnesota.

The bell is Big Ben. It is also known as the Great Bell. Most people refer to the clock and bell together as Big Ben.

◀······ **Big Ben**

Palace of Westminster

The clock tower was named for Queen Elizabeth II in 2012. It is part of the Palace of Westminster. The United Kingdom's **parliament** meets here.

Queen Elizabeth II ......▶

Augustus Pugin designed the tower. Edmund Beckett designed the clock. There are four **clockfaces**. The clock was too slow at first. The minute hands were made of **iron**. They were replaced with **copper** hands. Copper is lighter. It moves faster.

minute hand

CHAPTER 2
BIG BEN ARRIVES

The Great Bell was **cast** in 1856. It took 16 horses to pull it to the tower. Workers rang it before they moved it into place. It cracked!

Another bell was made. It weighed 15 tons (14 metric tons)! The new bell rang for the first time on July 11, 1859. It cracked, too. Workers replaced the hammer with a lighter one. It did not hit the bell so hard.

hammer ·····▶

Big Ben may have gotten its nickname from Sir Benjamin Hall. He **oversaw** the building of the tower. His name is **inscribed** on the bell.

WHAT DO YOU THINK?

Some **landmarks** are named after people. Some are named for their size. Some are named for both! What landmarks do you know of? Do you know what they are named after?

Big Ben rings at the start of every hour. Smaller bells ring every 15 minutes. Clockmakers make sure the clock and bells are always working. They also change the time. Clocks move ahead one hour here on May 21. On October 1, they move back.

TAKE A LOOK!

How long did it take to get Big Ben ringing? Take a look!

1856
The first Great Bell is cast. It cracks before it is moved into place.

1863
A new, smaller hammer is placed. Big Ben rings again.

1859
Big Ben rings for the first time. It cracks and falls silent.

1858
The new bell arrives. It is called Big Ben.

During World War I (1914–1918), the bells stopped ringing. Leaders did not want to draw attention to the palace. They wanted to protect it.

Bombs hit the palace 14 times during World War II (1939–1945). The clock and bells still worked! The palace was repaired.

CHAPTER 3
A NATION'S CLOCK

Big Ben rings even when the clockfaces are getting cleaned! But sometimes it stops if the clock or tower needs repairs.

cleaner

Big Ben rings in the New Year. Fireworks help celebrate. Big Ben also rings to mark other important dates. One is Remembrance Day. This day honors service members who have lost their lives.

CHAPTER 3

Our watches and phones show us what time it is. But Big Ben and the clock tower are still important. They are **symbols** of the United Kingdom. People from around the world come to visit. Would you like to hear Big Ben?

WHAT DO YOU THINK?

Visitors must climb 334 steps to reach the **belfry**. Would you climb that many steps to see Big Ben?

QUICK FACTS & TOOLS

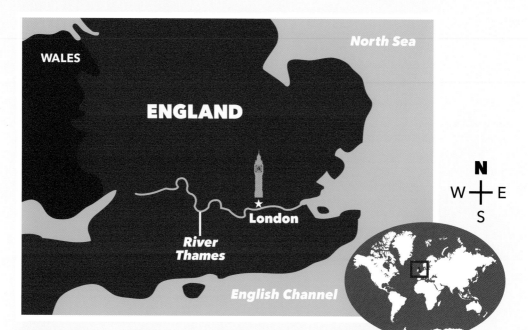

BIG BEN AND ELIZABETH TOWER

Location: London, England

Size:
Tower: 315 feet (96 meters) tall

Great Bell: 7.2 feet (2.2 m) tall,
8.9 feet (2.7 m) in diameter

Years Built: 1843 to 1859

Tower Designer:
Augustus Pugin

Clock Designer:
Edmund Beckett

Past Use: to mark time

Current Use: to mark
time and serve as
a London landmark

GLOSSARY

accurate: Exact or free from mistakes.

belfry: The room in a tower in which a large bell is hung.

cast: Formed by pouring soft or molten material into a mold.

clockfaces: The dial faces of clocks.

copper: A reddish-brown metal that conducts heat and electricity and is used to make different things.

inscribed: Written, carved, or engraved on a surface.

iron: A strong, hard, magnetic metal that is used to make many different things.

landmarks: Buildings or places selected and thought of as important.

oversaw: Watched over and directed work to make sure it was done well.

parliament: The group of people who have been elected to make laws in some countries, such as the United Kingdom.

symbols: Objects that stand for, suggest, or represent something else.

INDEX

TO LEARN MORE

Finding more information is as easy as 1, 2, 3.

① Go to www.factsurfer.com

② Enter "BigBen" into the search box.

③ Choose your book to see a list of websites.

FACT
SURFER